AGE IS just a Number

AGE IS just a Number

More Than **150** Quotations on Aging with Humor and Style

Illustrations by Phil Marden

Get Creative 6

Get Creative 6

An imprint of Mixed Media Resources
104 West 27th Street
New York, NY 10001

Connect with us on Facebook at facebook.com/getcreative6

Senior Editor MICHELLE BREDESON
Art Director IRENE LEDWITH
Managing Editor LAURA COOKE
. . . .
Vice President TRISHA MALCOLM
Chief Operating Officer CAROLINE KILMER
Production Manager DAVID JOINNIDES
President ART JOINNIDES
Chairman JAY STEIN

Library of Congress Cataloging-in-Publication Data available upon request.

Manufactured in China

1 3 5 7 9 10 8 6 4 2

First Edition

Live Forever . . . Or Die Trying!

"Old age isn't so bad when you consider the alternative," especially when you can draw on the wit and wisdom of the ages to age with grace, humor, and optimism. *Age Is Just a Number* gathers together more than 150 quotations from writers, actors, athletes, humorists, politicians, and other great minds and entertainers from bygone eras to today. The quotes range from the irreverent ("Do not worry about avoiding temptation. As you grow older it will avoid you.") to the whimsical ("Growing old is mandatory; growing up is optional.") to the sage ("The more sand has escaped from the hourglass of our life, the clearer we should see through it."). The inspiring quotations in this entertaining collection will have you convinced that "the shady side of fifty" is the best time of your life. As Robert Browning said, "Grow old along with me! The best is yet to be!"

You are never too old to set
another goal or to dream
a new dream.

C. S. LEWIS
British writer

Memory is the first casualty of middle age, if I remember correctly.

CANDICE BERGEN

American actress

At age 20, we worry about what others think of us.

At age 40, we don't care what they think of us.

At age 60, we discover they haven't been thinking of us at all.

ANN LANDERS

American advice columnist

Age appears to be best in four things: old wood to burn, old wine to drink, old friends to trust, and old authors to read.

FRANCIS BACON

English philosopher, statesman, and scientist

*As we grow old,
the beauty steals inward.*

RALPH WALDO EMERSON

American essayist, poet, and philosopher

Animal lover that I am,
a cougar I am not.

BETTY WHITE
American actress and comedian

Men do not quit playing
because they grow old;
they grow old because
they quit playing.

OLIVER WENDELL HOLMES SR.

American physician and poet

And the beauty of a woman, with passing years only grows!

AUDREY HEPBURN

British actress and humanitarian

I'm saving that rocker for
the day when I feel
as old as I really am.

DWIGHT D. EISENHOWER
U.S. President and general

To find joy in work is to discover the fountain of youth.

PEARL S. BUCK
American writer and Nobel laureate

We are always the same age inside.

GERTRUDE STEIN

American novelist, poet, and playwright

You'll never see a U-Haul behind a hearse. . . . I can't take it with me, and neither can you. It's not how much you have but what you do with what you have.

DENZEL WASHINGTON
American actor and director

*The greatest thing
in life is to keep
your mind young.*

HENRY FORD

American businessman

People ask me what I'd most appreciate getting for my eighty-seventh birthday. I tell them, a paternity suit.

GEORGE BURNS

American comedian, actor, and writer

To keep the heart unwrinkled, to be hopeful, kindly, cheerful, reverent—that is to triumph over old age.

THOMAS BAILEY ALDRICH
American writer, poet, and critic

The idea is to die young as late as possible.

ASHLEY MONTAGU

British-American anthropologist

If wrinkles must be written on our brows, let them not be written upon the heart. The spirit should never grow old.

JAMES A. GARFIELD

U.S. President

Knowing how to age and not being afraid of aging is very healthy.

EVELYN LAUDER

Austrian-American businesswoman and philanthropist

Age is just a number. It's totally irrelevant unless, of course, you happen to be a bottle of wine.

JOAN COLLINS
English actress and author

Something pretty. . . that's just the surface. People worry so much about aging, but you look younger if you don't worry about it.

JEANNE MOREAU
French actress, singer, and director

If youth knew;
if age could.

SIGMUND FREUD
Austrian neurologist and psychoanalyst

Age does not bring you wisdom, age brings you wrinkles.

ESTELLE GETTY
American actress and comedian

It's not how old you are,
it's how you are old.

JULES RENARD
French author

I must be careful not to get trapped in the past. That's why I tend to forget my songs.

MICK JAGGER

English singer-songwriter and musician

Nobody grows old merely by living a number of years. We grow old by deserting our ideals. Years may wrinkle the skin, but to give up enthusiasm wrinkles the soul.

SAMUEL ULLMAN

American businessman, poet, and humanitarian

Age does not protect you
from love. But love, to some
extent, protects you from age.

ANAÏS NIN
French-American writer

Preparation for old age should begin
not later than one's teens. A life which
is empty of purpose until 65 will not
suddenly become filled on retirement.

DWIGHT L. MOODY
American evangelist and publisher

The wisest are the most annoyed at the loss of time.

DANTE ALIGHIERI

Italian poet

I'll quit competing when my heart quits beating.

MICHAEL JORDAN

American basketball player

I never have a sense of finishing up, just new things beginning. When I die, they're going to carry me off a stage.

ANGELA LANSBURY
English-American-Irish actress

I think your whole life shows in your face and you should be proud of that.

LAUREN BACALL

American actress

What I look forward to is continued immaturity followed by death.

DAVE BARRY
American author and columnist

With mirth and laughter let old wrinkles come.

WILLIAM SHAKESPEARE
English poet, actor, and playwright

*Life goes by fast.
Enjoy it. Calm down.
It's all funny. Next.
Everyone gets so upset
about the wrong things.*

JOAN RIVERS

American comedian, actress, and television host

Let us never know what old age is. Let us know the happiness time brings, not count the years.

AUSONIUS

Roman poet and teacher

Don't let aging get you down. It's too hard to get back up.

JOHN WAGNER
British-American comics writer

You don't stop laughing when you grow old, you grow old when you stop laughing.

GEORGE BERNARD SHAW

Irish playwright, critic, and Nobel laureate

It is a mistake to regard age as a downhill grade toward dissolution. The reverse is true. As one grows older, one climbs with surprising strides.

GEORGE SAND

French novelist

The 2,000-Year-Old Man's Secrets of Longevity:

1. Don't run for a bus—there'll always be another.

2. Never, ever touch fried food.

3. Stay out of a Ferrari or any other small Italian car.

4. Eat fruit—a nectarine—even a rotten plum is good.

MEL BROOKS

American actor, writer, director, and comedian

We can grow gracefully, or gorgeously. I pick both.

DIANE KEATON
American actress, director, and producer

As the arteries grow hard,
the heart grows soft.

H. L. MENCKEN

American journalist and satirist

Now that I'm over sixty, I'm veering toward respectability.

SHELLEY WINTERS
American actress

Men are like wine—
some turn to vinegar,
but the best improve
with age.

POPE JOHN XXIII

After thirty, a body has a mind of its own.

BETTE MIDLER
American singer and actress

Life is like a hot bath. It feels good while you're in it, but the longer you stay, the more wrinkled you get.

JIM DAVIS

Cartoonist

In childhood be modest,
in youth temperate,
in adulthood just,
and in old age prudent.

SOCRATES

Greek philosopher

Grow old along with me!
The best is yet to be.

ROBERT BROWNING

English poet and playwright

Old age transfigures
or fossilizes.

MARIE VON EBNER-ESCHENBACH
Austrian writer

The afternoon knows what the morning never suspected.

ROBERT FROST

American poet

You know you're getting old
when the candles cost more
than the cake.

BOB HOPE

American actor and comedian

No experience is wasted.
Everything in life is happening
to grow you up, to fill you up,
to help you become more of
who you were created to be.

OPRAH WINFREY

American television host, actress, and philanthropist

You know you're getting old when all the names in your black book have M.D. after them.

HARRISON FORD
American actor and producer

The greatest potential for growth and self-realization exists in the second half of life.

CARL JUNG

Swiss psychiatrist and psychoanalyst

If you're going to get old, you might as well get as old as you can get.

WALLACE STEGNER
American writer

Life is very short . . .
but I would like to live four
times and if I could, I would
set out to do no other
things than I am seeking
now to do.

WILLIAM MERRITT CHASE
American painter

I think you should be a child for as long as you can. I have been successful for 74 years being able to do that. Don't rush into adulthood, it isn't all that much fun.

BOB NEWHART
American comedian and actor

Age is not all decay; it is the ripening, the swelling, of the fresh life within, that withers and bursts the husk.

GEORGE MACDONALD
Scottish author, poet, and minister

Nature gives you the face you have at twenty; it is up to you to merit the face you have at fifty.

COCO CHANEL

French fashion designer

Live as if you were to die tomorrow. Learn as if you were to live forever.

MAHATMA GANDHI

Indian activist

I will never give in to old age until I become old. And I'm not old yet!

TINA TURNER
American singer, dancer, and actress

In the end, it's not
the years in your life
that count. It's the
life in your years.

ABRAHAM LINCOLN
U.S. President

Never tease an old dog; he might have one bite left.

ROBERT A. HEINLEIN

American science-fiction writer

Life's just one great journey.
It's a road we travel as we
go from point A to point B.
What makes that journey
worthwhile is the people we
choose to travel with . . .

DR. SEUSS
American children's author and artist

No one can avoid aging, but aging productively is something else.

KATHARINE GRAHAM
American newspaper publisher

The really frightening thing about middle age is the knowledge that you'll grow out of it.

DORIS DAY

American actress, singer, and animal-rights activitist

My faith demands that I do whatever I can, wherever I am, whenever I can, for as long as I can with whatever I have to try to make a difference.

JIMMY CARTER
U.S. President

The old begin to complain
of the conduct of the young
when they themselves are
no longer able to set a
bad example.

FRANÇOIS DE LA ROCHEFOUCAULD
French author

I'm happy to report that
my inner child is still
ageless.

JAMES BROUGHTON
American poet and filmmaker

Youth is the gift of nature, but age is a work of art.

STANISLAW JERZY LEC
Polish poet

My mission in life is not merely to survive, but to thrive; and to do so with some passion, some compassion, some humor, and some style.

MAYA ANGELOU
American poet, memoirist, and activist

Some things get better with age. Like me.

KEITH RICHARDS

English musician and songwriter

For age is opportunity no less
Than youth itself, though in
another dress,
And as the evening twilight
fades away
The sky is filled with stars,
invisible by day.

HENRY WADSWORTH LONGFELLOW
American poet

What counts in life is not the mere fact that we have lived. It is what difference we have made to the lives of others that will determine the significance of the life we lead.

NELSON MANDELA

Anti-apartheid revolutionary and President of South Africa

I believe that you're here on Earth for a short time, and while you're here, you shouldn't forget it.

BEA ARTHUR

American actress, comedian, and singer

Always focus on the front windshield and not the rearview mirror.

COLIN POWELL
American statesman and four-star general

I'm at an age when my back goes out more than I do.

PHYLLIS DILLER

American actress and comedian

The older I get, the more clearly I remember things that never happened.

MARK TWAIN

American writer and humorist

Stay curious, keep learning and keep growing. And always strive to be more interested than interesting.

JANE FONDA

American actress, writer, and activist

No spring nor summer beauty
hath such grace as I have
seen in one autumnal face.

JOHN DONNE
English poet

You can only perceive real beauty in a person as they get older.

ANOUK AIMÉE

French actress

To know how to grow old is the master work of wisdom, and one of the most difficult chapters in the great art of living.

HERMAN MELVILLE
American novelist and poet

It is never too late to be
what you might have been.

GEORGE ELIOT
English writer

Forty is the old age of youth;
fifty the youth of old age.

VICTOR HUGO
French poet, novelist, and dramatist

Laughter is pleasant,
but the exertion at my age
is too much for me.

THOMAS LOVE PEACOCK

English novelist and poet

I fear waking up one morning and finding out my life was all for nothing. We're here for a reason. I believe a bit of the reason is to throw little torches out to lead people through the dark.

WHOOPI GOLDBERG
American actress, comedian, and television host

A man is not old until regrets
take the place of dreams.

JOHN BARRYMORE
American actor

Here is the test to find whether your mission on Earth is finished: If you're alive, it isn't.

RICHARD BACH

American writer

I am getting to an age when
I can only enjoy the last
sport left. It is called hunting
for your spectacles.

EDWARD GREY, 1st Viscount Grey of Fallodon
British statesman

None are so old as those who have outlived enthusiasm.

HENRY DAVID THOREAU

American essayist, poet, and philosopher

One of the few advantages to not being beautiful is that one usually gets better-looking as one gets older. I am, in fact, at this very moment gaining my looks.

NORA EPHRON
American journalist, writer, and filmmaker

In youth we run into difficulties. In old age difficulties run into us.

BEVERLY SILLS
American opera singer

I'm like a good cheese.
I'm just getting moldy
enough to be interesting.

PAUL NEWMAN

American actor, director, entrepreneur,
and philanthropist

No man is ever old enough to know better.

HOLBROOK JACKSON

British journalist, writer, and publisher

To all, I would say how mistaken they are when they think that they stop falling in love when they grow old, without knowing that they grow old when they stop falling in love.

GABRIEL GARCÍA MÁRQUEZ

Colombian novelist, screenwriter, and journalist

Life should not be a journey to the grave with the intention of arriving safely in a pretty and well-preserved body, but rather to skid in broadside in a cloud of smoke, thoroughly used up, totally worn out, and loudly proclaiming "Wow! What a Ride!"

HUNTER S. THOMPSON
American journalist and author

Old age is no place
for sissies.

BETTE DAVIS
American actress

Growing old is mandatory;
growing up is optional.

CHILI DAVIS

Jamaican-American baseball player and coach

Old age is not a matter for sorrow. It is a matter for thanks if we have left our work done behind us.

THOMAS CARLYLE

Scottish philosopher, writer, historian, and mathematician

We are reminded that, in the fleeting time we have on this Earth, what matters is not wealth, or status, or power, or fame, but rather how well we have loved and what small part we have played in making the lives of other people better.

BARACK OBAMA
U.S. President

Aging is not lost youth
but a new stage of
opportunity and strength.

BETTY FRIEDAN

American writer, activist, and feminist

A man growing old
becomes a child again.

SOPHOCLES
Greek tragedian

I intend to live forever,

or die trying.

GROUCHO MARX

American comedian, actor, and writer

Those who love deeply never grow old; they may die of old age, but they die young.

BENJAMIN FRANKLIN

U.S. Founding Father

Age is strictly a case of mind over matter. If you don't mind, it doesn't matter.

JACK BENNY

Amerian comedian, actor, and violinist

There is a fountain of youth:
it is your mind, your talents,
the creativity you bring to your
life and the lives of people
you love. When you learn to
tap this source, you will truly
have defeated age.

SOPHIA LOREN
Italian actress

The secret of genius is to
carry the spirit of the child into
old age, which means never
losing your enthusiasm.

ALDOUS HUXLEY

English writer and philosopher

The more sand has escaped
from the hourglass of our life, the
clearer we should see through it.

NICCOLÒ MACHIAVELLI

Italian diplomat, politician, and writer

*Life is very short.
Insecurity is a
waste of time.*

DIANE VON FÜRSTENBERG

Belgian-American fashion designer

Cherish all your happy moments; they make a fine cushion for old age.

BOOTH TARKINGTON

American novelist and dramatist

Do not worry about avoiding
temptation. As you grow older
it will avoid you.

JOEY ADAMS
American comedian

I'm inspired by people who keep
on rolling, no matter their age.

JIMMY BUFFETT

American musician

Another belief of mine: that everyone else my age is an adult, whereas I am merely in disguise.

MARGARET ATWOOD

Canadian poet, novelist, and critic

Life can only be
understood backwards;
but it must be lived
forwards.

SØREN KIERKEGAARD

Danish philosopher

You have to stay in shape.
My grandmother, she started
walking five miles a day when she
was 60. She's 97 today and we
don't know where the hell she is.

ELLEN DEGENERES
American actress, comedian, and television host

If you have anything better to be doing when death overtakes you, get to work on that.

EPICTETUS

Greek Stoic philosopher

I'm at the age where food has taken the place of sex in my life. In fact, I've just had a mirror put over my kitchen table.

RODNEY DANGERFIELD
American comedian and actor

Do not grow old, no matter how long you live. Never cease to stand like curious children before the Great Mystery into which we were born.

ALBERT EINSTEIN
German physicist and Nobel laureate

I look forward to being older,
when what you look like
becomes less and less an issue
and what you are is the point.

SUSAN SARANDON
American actress and activist

Nothing is more responsible for the good old days than a bad memory.

FRANKLIN P. ADAMS

American columnist

There's many a good tune
played by an old banjo.

ANTHONY HOPKINS

Welsh actor

Life is long if it is full.

SENECA THE YOUNGER

Roman Stoic philosopher, dramatist, and satirist

I am learning all the time. The tombstone will be my diploma.

EARTHA KITT
American singer, actress, and activist

The great secret that all old people share is that you really haven't changed in seventy or eighty years. Your body changes, but you don't change at all. And that, of course, causes great confusion.

DORIS LESSING
British novelist, poet, playwright, and Nobel laureate

Of course, I continue to
play and to practice. I think
I would do so if I lived for
another hundred years.

PABLO CASALS
Spanish cellist, composer, and conductor

Always semi-retire, never retire.
Who wants to just sit somewhere?

ARETHA FRANKLIN

American singer and songwriter

I do the New York Times crossword puzzle every morning to keep the old grey matter ticking.

CAROL BURNETT

American actress, writer, and comedian

A man who views the world the same at fifty as he did at twenty has wasted thirty years of his life.

MUHAMMAD ALI

American boxer and activist

Except for an occasional heart attack I feel as young as I ever did.

ROBERT BENCHLEY

American humorist

Yesterday I was clever, so I wanted to change the world. Today I am wise, so I am changing myself.

RUMI

Persian poet and mystic

You have to embrace getting older. Life is precious and when you have lost a lot of people, you realize each day is a gift.

MERYL STREEP

American actress

A stockbroker urged me to buy a stock that would triple its value every year. I told him, "At my age, I don't even buy green bananas."

CLAUDE PEPPER
American politician

You're only young
once, but you can be
immature forever.

GERMAINE GREER

Australian writer, intellectual, and feminist

Old age, believe me, is a good and pleasant thing. It is true you are gently shouldered off the stage, but then you are given such a comfortable front stall as spectator.

CONFUCIUS
Chinese teacher and philosopher

They tell you that you'll lose
your mind when you grow older.
What they don't tell you is that
you won't miss it very much.

MALCOLM COWLEY
American writer, historian, poet, and literary critic

Old age is a special problem
for me because I've never
been able to shed the
mental image I have of
myself—a lad of about 19.

E. B. WHITE
American writer

True terror is to wake up one morning and discover that your high school class is running the country.

KURT VONNEGUT

American writer

Age is not important unless you're a cheese.

HELEN HAYES

American actress

Life is not a spectator sport.
If you're going to spend your
whole life in the grandstand just
watching what goes on, in my
opinion you're wasting your life.

JACKIE ROBINSON
American baseball player

I have a lifetime appointment and I intend to serve it. I expect to die at 110, shot by a jealous husband.

THURGOOD MARSHALL
Supreme Court justice

The secret of staying young
is to live honestly, eat slowly,
and lie about your age.

LUCILLE BALL

American actress and comedian

Education is the best provision for old age.

ARISTOTLE

Greek philosopher and scientist

The trouble with retirement is that you never get a day off.

ABE LEMONS

American basketball player and coach

Growing old is no more than a bad habit which a busy person has no time to form.

ANDRÉ MAUROIS
French author

It takes a long time
to become young.

PABLO PICASSO

Spanish artist

You have to be able to look back at your life and say, "Yeah, that was fun."

SAMMY DAVIS JR.
American singer, actor, and dancer

"Age" is the acceptance
of a term of years.
But maturity is
the glory of years.

MARTHA GRAHAM

American dancer and choreographer

*Laughter is timeless,
imagination has no age,
and dreams are forever.*

WALT DISNEY

American entrepreneur and animator

It is best as one grows older to strip oneself of possessions, to shed oneself downward like a tree, to be almost wholly earth before one dies.

SYLVIA TOWNSEND WARNER

English novelist and poet

You don't get to be old bein' no fool.

RICHARD PRYOR

American comedian and actor

Old age isn't so bad when
you consider the alternative.

MAURICE CHEVALIER

French actor and singer

As we grow older, our capacity for enjoyment shrinks, but not our appetite for it.

MIGNON McCLAUGHLIN

American journalist and author

Old age is like
everything else.
To make a success
of it, you've got to
start young.

THEODORE ROOSEVELT

U.S. President

As you get older three things happen. The first is your memory goes, and I can't remember the other two.

NORMAN WISDOM

English actor, comedian, and singer-songwriter

It is sad to grow old
but nice to ripen.

BRIGITTE BARDOT
French actress, dancer, model, and activist

The value of old age depends upon the person who reaches it. To some men of early performance it is useless. To others, who are late to develop, it just enables them to finish the job.

THOMAS HARDY
English novelist and poet

How old would you be if you didn't know how old you are?

SATCHEL PAIGE

American baseball player

You show me anyone who's lived to over seventy and you show me a fighter—someone who's got the will to live.

AGATHA CHRISTIE

English mystery writer

I don't mind growing old.
I'm just not used to it.

VICTOR BORGE

Danish-American comedian, conductor, and pianist

No man was ever so completely skilled in the conduct of life, as not to receive new information from age and experience.

JONATHAN SWIFT

Anglo-Irish satirist, essayist, and poet

Youth is when you're allowed to
stay up late on New Year's Eve.
Middle age is when you're forced to.

BILL VAUGHAN
American columnist and author

The great thing about getting older is that you don't lose all the other ages you've been.

MADELEINE L'ENGLE

American writer

I didn't get old on purpose, it just happened. If you're lucky, it could happen to you.

ANDY ROONEY

American radio and television writer

Even now, at 82 years old, if I don't learn something every day, you know what I think? It's a day lost.

B. B. KING
American singer, guitarist, and songwriter

The heyday of woman's life is the shady side of fifty.

ELIZABETH CADY STANTON

American suffragist, social activist, and abolitionist

As a graduate of the Zsa Zsa Gabor School of Creative Mathematics, I honestly do not know how old I am.

ERMA BOMBECK
American humorist

Musicians don't retire;
they stop when there's no
more music in them.

LOUIS ARMSTRONG
American trumpeter, composer, and singer

You can get old pretty young if you don't take care of yourself.

YOGI BERRA

American baseball player and coach

I personally stay away from natural foods. At my age I need all the preservatives I can get.

W. C. FIELDS
American comedian, actor, and writer

About the Illustrator

After studying animal behavior, Phil Marden moved to New York City, where he worked as a layout artist and graphic designer. There, he honed his skills as an illustrator for publishing, advertising, commercials, television shows, and movies. He has illustrated regular columns in the *New York Times*, the *Boston Globe*, *Spy*, *Self*, and other publications. He lives in Portland, Oregon.

Index